A DINOSAUR ALPHABET

The

of Prehistoric Beasts!

by Michelle Hasselius

illustrated by Clair Rossiter

PICTURE WINDOW BOOKS
a capstone imprint

 **is for Ankylosaurus.**

Ankylosaurus swung its heavy club tail at hungry predators like Tyrannosaurus rex. **BAM!** The strong armor on Ankylosaurus' skin protected it from sharp teeth and claws.

(ANG-kuh-lo-SAWR-us)

B is for Brachiosaurus.

Brachiosaurus was **BIG!** It was taller than the trees!
This giant dino was one of the largest animals ever to walk on Earth.

(BRACK-ee-uh-SAWR-us)

 **C is for Coelophysis.**

Coelophysis was a small, speedy dinosaur. It weighed about as much as a border collie. The dinosaur could chase after tasty lizards or run away from predators.

(SEE-lo-FY-sis)

D is for Dracorex.

Dracorex looked like a spiky-headed dragon. The dinosaur's full name means "dragon king of Hogwarts." It was named after Hogwarts School in the Harry Potter books.

(DRAY-co-rex)

E is for Euoplocephalus.

Euoplocephalus was ready for battle! It had sharp spikes down its back and armor on its head and body. Euoplocephalus even had armor on its eyelids!

(YOU-oh-plo-SEF-ah-lus)

F is for Futalognkosaurus.

Futalognkosaurus was a very *loooong* dinosaur. It measured 100 feet (30 meters) from its tail to its head. That's longer than a basketball court.

(FOO-tah-lon-koh-SAWR-us)

G is for Gallimimus.

Gallimimus could really go! The dashing dinosaur could run up to 30 miles (48 kilometers) per hour. That's as fast as a tiger can run today. **Zoom!**

(GAL-ih-MY-mus)

H is for Huayangosaurus.

Huayangosaurus was one of the first stegosaurs. It was much smaller than its famous relative, Stegosaurus.

1st

(hwi-YANG-uh-SAWR-us)

I is for Iguanodon.

Iguanodon had five fingers on each front foot. But they didn't look like your fingers. The dinosaur's three middle fingers were stuck together. Instead of thumbs, Iguanodon had long, sharp spikes.

(ih-GWAN-oh-dahn)

J is for Janenschia.

Janenschia was a giant plant-eating dinosaur. It used its long neck to pluck the leaves off the tops of tall trees.

(ja-NEN-she-ah)

 **is for Kentrosaurus.**

Kentrosaurus was a stegosaur, like Huayangosaurus. Kentrosaurus had two rows of strong plates that went halfway down its back. Then the plates turned to spikes, which ran down its tail.

(KEN-tro-SAWR-us)

L is for Leptoceratops.

Leptoceratops was a member of the horned dinosaurs. It and some of the other "horned" dinosaurs didn't actually have horns. Leptoceratops had a frill on its head.

(LEP-tuh-SER-uh-tops)

 **is for Megalosaurus.**

Megalosaurus was a big meat-eater that walked on two legs. Its sharp, jagged teeth looked like a saw. Megalosaurus was one of the first dinosaurs ever discovered.

(MEG-ah-lo-SAWR-us)

N is for Neovenator.

Neovenator was a deadly hunter. The dinosaur had three sharp claws on each foot. It chased after dinosaurs and attacked. **Watch out!**

(NEE-oh-vuh-NAY-tur)

O is for Oviraptor.

Oviraptor looked like a bird. It had feathers and a hard beak. But the dinosaur couldn't fly. Instead it ran on its two back legs, like an ostrich.

(OH-vih-RAP-tor)

P is for Protoceratops.

Protoceratops had a sharp beak and bony frill. Fossils from this and another dinosaur, Velociraptor, were found in Mongolia. Scientists think they were in the middle of a battle when a sandstorm covered them both with sand.

(PRO-to-SER-uh-tops)

17

 **is for Qianzhousaurus.**

Qianzhousaurus was a carnivore with a long snout. It was so long and pointed, scientists call this dinosaur "Pinocchio Rex."

(shee-AHN-zhoo-SAWR-us)

18

R is for Rajasaurus.

Rajasaurus' name means "prince lizard." This meat-eater didn't live in a castle. Rajasaurus did have a small crest on its head that looked like a crown.

(RAH-jah-SAWR-us)

 **S** **is for Stegosaurus.**

Stegosaurus is the most well-known stegosaur. Stegosaurus' brain was the size of a walnut, but its body was as big as a bus!

(STEG-uh-SAWR-us)

T is for Tyrannosaurus rex.

Tyrannosaurus rex may be the most popular dinosaur. It had a huge head full of razor-sharp teeth. Scientists think the dinosaur could eat up to 500 pounds (227 kilograms) of meat in one bite. **Chomp!**

(ty-RAN-uh-SAWR-us REX)

U is for Utahraptor.

Utahraptor is the biggest raptor discovered so far. It had a deadly, 9-inch (23-centimeter) claw on each foot. This hunter sunk its claw into even bigger dinosaurs, like Iguanodon.

(YU-tah-RAP-tor)

V is for Velociraptor.

Velociraptor was about the size of a small turkey. Even though it was small, the raptor was dangerous. Velociraptor had sharp teeth and a curved claw on each foot. Velociraptor may have even hunted in packs to kill larger dinosaurs.

(vuh-LOSS-uh-RAP-tor)

23

 **is for Wuerhosaurus.**

Wuerhosaurus was one of the last stegosaurs on Earth.
It lived in Asia more than 110 million years ago.

(woo-EHR-ho-SAWR-us)

X is for Xenoceratops.

Xenoceratops' name means "alien horned face." But it's not from another world. This big dinosaur had two long horns over its eyes and little horns all around its frill.

(ZEE-no-SER-uh-tops)

Y is for Yi qi.

Yi qi was about the size of a pigeon. It had wings like a bat, but it couldn't fly. Instead the dinosaur glided through the air.

(EE CHEE)

26

Z is for Zhongyuansaurus.

Zhongyuansaurus was the only ankylosaur that didn't have a club tail. But it could still protect itself with its hard armor.

(ZHONG-yu-an-SAWR-us)

Glossary

ankylosaur—a group of plant-eating dinosaurs from the Cretaceous Period with thick bodies and bony armor; Ankylosaurus was an ankylosaur

armor—bones, scales, and skin that some animals have on their bodies for protection

beak—the hard front part of a bird's mouth; some dinosaurs had beaks

carnivore—an animal that eats only meat

fossil—the remains or traces of an animal or plant from millions of years ago, preserved in rock

frill—a large, bony plate that grows from the back of an animal's skull

glide—to move through the air in a controlled way but without power

herbivore—an animal that eats only plants

plate—a flat, bony growth on an animal

predator—an animal that hunts other animals for food

sandstorm—a strong windstorm that blows sand around

snout—the long front part of an animal's head; the snout includes the nose, mouth, and jaws

spike—a sharp, pointy part of an animal

stegosaur—a group of plant-eating dinosaurs that walked on four legs and had plates and spikes on their bodies; Stegosaurus was a stegosaur

Read More

Crowther, Robert. *Robert Crowther's Pop-Up Dinosaur ABC.*
Somerville, Mass.: Candlewick Press, 2015.

Werner, Sharon, and Sarah Forss. *Alphasaurs and Other Prehistoric Types.* Maplewood, N.J.: Blue Apple Books, 2011.

West, David. *Dinosaur Alphabet.* I Learn with Dinosaurs.
New York: Crabtree, 2013.

Internet Sites

FactHound offers a safe, fun way to find Internet sites related to this book. All of the sites on FactHound have been researched by our staff.

Here's all you do:

Visit *www.facthound.com*

Type in this code: 9781479568840

Super-cool stuff! Check out projects, games and lots more at
www.capstonekids.com

Index

Editor: Gillia Olson
Designer: Ashlee Suker
Art Director: Nathan Gassman
Production Specialist: Katy LaVigne
The illustrations in this book were created digitally.

Picture Window Books are published by Capstone,
1710 Roe Crest Drive, North Mankato, Minnesota 56003
www.mycapstone.com

Library of Congress Cataloging-in-Publication Data
Library of Congress Cataloging-in-Publication data is available on the
Library of Congress website.

ISBN: 978-1-4795-6884-0 (library binding)
ISBN: 978-1-4795-6912-0 (paperback)
ISBN: 978-1-4795-6924-3 (ebook PDF)

Printed and bound in the United States of America.
012018   011009R

Other Titles in this Series

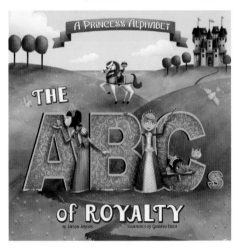